SKRAG

SKRAG

DAVID ARNASON

To Mot
With admiration
for all her wonderful
translations of art on
the CBC.

David Arn

TURNSTONE PRESS

© 1987 David Arnason

Published with the assistance of the Manitoba
Arts Council and the Canada Council.

Turnstone Press
607-99 King Street
Winnipeg, Manitoba
Canada R3B 1H7

This book was typeset by Communigraphics and
printed by Hignell Printing Limited for
Turnstone Press.

Printed in Canada.

Cover design: Robert MacDonald

Some of these poems have appeared in *Arts Manitoba/
Border Crossings, CV/2, Dinosaur Review, Grain, The
Manitoban, Northward Journal,* and *Draft: An Anthology of
Prairie Poetry.*

Canadian Cataloguing in Publication Data

Arnason, David, 1940-
  Skrag

  Poems.
  ISBN 0-88801-114-8

  I. Title.

PS8551.R627S5 1987   C811'.54   C87-098018-1
PR9199.3.A75S5 1987

For Brian Boszko,
1962-1985

Contents

SKRAG

Skrag   killer of midnight chickens
relentless father of his enemies and lovers
scourge of the lazy and the unaware
chief constable   walker of dark roads
giver of pleasure   nighttime singer
surveyor and mapper   reader of musk and balm
master of bush and field   Skrag
flicks an offending ear   scratches
an itchy flank   stretches out to sleep
in the full glow of the admiring sun

Skrag   watches the wary cats
offensive in their insular
sureness of speed   castled
in the safety of the barn
moving out to territory
he has forbidden them   Skrag
stretches stiff legs   ambles
toward the creek   angling
for position   too late
cat with his coward's luck
a grey streak   Skrag
misses by an inch
at the barn door   Skrag
watches the geese
moving to forbidden territory

Skrag   slave to unyielding love
perks to the whistle   runs to the call
here Skrags   come boy   nuzzles
for the debased joy of the hand
on the head   the scratch on the ear
there can never be enough of this
Skrag   moaning low in his throat
his mind empty of cats and geese
tail wags the abasements of love
this man   this frail giver of love
taker of love   vulnerable and weak
always in need of protection
blind to death on the wind
unaware of the danger everywhere
Skrag   circling and returning
the loving hand   the peril everywhere

Skrag   knows the joy of the kill
fur or feathers   blood hot in the mouth
mice by the hundreds   rabbits   rats
chickens skunks gophers   groundhogs
badgers and once a deer   caught
in a late March storm   Skrag
lay with his mouth in the seeping
blood   the torn entrails   now
when he dreams he dreams of deer

Skrag   leaps from the kick
of the old one   the silent one
circles him cautiously   knowing
the touch of the cane   the smell
of tobacco spit in the hair   Skrag
leaving him there   lopes to the bridge
he has things to do in the south pasture

Skrag   on a March morning
twitches awake   alarms clang
in his head   a message in musk
on the balmy air   Skrag
it says   come to me my lover
this is my hour and you must be there
three miles   and Skrag is first
to arrive as usual   settles
on the driveway near the door
then the other gentlemen callers arrive
lifting their tails so Skrag
can read their calling cards
then the opened door and she's there
Skrag is first   hard hump
bitch with her head cocked
looking over her shoulder
she's young but Skrag likes them young
likes them old too

Skrag   relentless biter of tires is chained
to the shed for his sins   Skrag
howls out his moonsong to the blazing noon
barks his dismay to the unattending trees
arrogant cats strut past the end of his chain
the geese are in the garden   eating the peas
cows have slipped the fence
and are walking the road
rabbits skip at the edge of the bush
Skrag   howls his dismay   disorder
is loosed on the world   licence
and chaos   and then of course a storm

Skrag   cynical philosopher
broods on the imperfect world
full of cats and geese
and endless disobedient cows
to be fetched night and morning
considers the nature of love
the hand on the head   the chirp
and the whistle   Skrag climbs
from his bed of straw   weighing
the exigencies of lust
against the responsibilities
of state   and wanders off down the road
in whatever direction

something wrong   Skrag knows it
before his pads crunch on the driveway snow
in the barn   the old one   death
heavy on the cold December air   lights
in the house   Skrag   pads to the barn door
slips through an opening   finds him
in the third stall   licks at his hand
quick licks at the cooling blood
the gaping wound   circles the shotgun
in the straw   wrong   something is wrong
outside to the mound by the dugout   Skrag
howls at the moon   blood
warm in his pulsing throat

Skrag   meticulous banker of bones
checks his supplies   under the shed
down by the creek   behind the barn
Skrag does his accounts   where
did he bury last week   where will
be safe today   better lost than taken
there is never enough to go around

Skrag   nuzzler of crotches
shameless thief of love
rolls on his back for the guests
see   she says   the sweet-smelling one
see how he likes his belly tickled   Skrag
feels his erection grow as she rubs
the pink tip cool in the open air
runs for the thrown stick   stands
on his hind legs   plays dead   Skrag
the immoral   the shameless one

Skrag   on a May morning
bright as pain   limbers
his muscles in a gentle lope
loops by the sleeping farmhouse
runs   runs to the correction line
his legs a lengthening
his body a rolling motion
wind in his eyes and fur
Skrag   philosopher king   knows
that the only joy is the body's joy

Skrag   defender of the one true faith
barks his sharp anger to the strangers
at the gas barrel on a dark December night
snaps at the heels of the fumbling farmboys
chases their half-ton to the end of the lane
Skrag   theolog of the north forty knows
that bright or dark in the reeling world
everything is owned

Skrag   singer of nighttime songs
is tuning his instrument   short
barks to the rising moon   long
slow glissando rising and falling
on the summer air   sharp cries
from a darkened window   shutup Skrags
get to sleep   Skrag doesn't care
he's heard it all before   chained
to the shed Skrag fashions another note
that will mean an end to chains

Skrag   wakes to the pattering rain
on the roof of the barn   cows moo
during milking   a kitten plays
with Skrag's paws   Skrag does not move
he lies in his bed of straw all through
the dust-filled emptiness of noon
the bustle of evening chores   what's
the matter Skrags   a little under the weather
and the quick pat on the head   Skrag
lies immobile in the gathering dusk
some days the world must take care of itself

Skrag   is fencing his fields
marking   fencepost willow and birch
extending a boundary here
retreating there   Skrag
calls to the man who hammers and sweats
see   it is safe here beyond barbed wire
these are the edges   but the man
continues stringing the frail wire
that anything can slip over or under

Skrag   restless scholar of the wind
reads his morning paper   rain
there will be rain   he smells anger
in the house   one of the cows is sick
somewhere to the north are horses
Skrag   in the grey dawn stretches
it will be a day without cats

Skrag   leaps to the whistle
the call   here Skrags   come boy
good fella   his limp leg dangling
his eyes blurred with pus   Skrag
sees the man only dimly   but he reads
danger on the damp fall air   Skrag
hurries for the hunt   he will flush
partridge and grouse by the creek
rabbits at the edge of the bush
he stares up the barrel at the aiming eye
Skrag learns   in the last triggered synapse
of his exploding brain   the final
meaning of love

THE COTTAGE POEMS

Willow Island, June

Waves do no violence to the rocks
they break on, or if they do,
the measure is too large to matter,
but the dead moths, the body of a gull
rotting on the sand are another thing.

And so the island sun that rises
and sets over water is witness
to many kinds of loss. Decay
is no simple thing, this or that.

I caught a dragon-fly carefully
in my hands (it had slipped in
through the screen) and released it.

I could have crushed it as I would a fly
and I might not have cared much. Yet

the rotting gull, the pile of moths
by my cottage door are not my fault
or anyone's though some would have it so.

And so the water that gives birth to
and buries the sun is not responsible
for the decay of rocks. A moral world
is more than who did what. Much more.

It is another thing entirely to say
why I should free a dragon-fly. Still
since you are here beside me I can say
I love you. That much is true and known.
The rest is not as easy. Waves break stone.

A Song for Carol

Brown rushes root in the cracked
and crystal ice on the far side
of the ditch. Wood smoke is sharp
on the still fall air, surprising
coots and teal in the lagoon.
Late seagulls and casual crows
drift dark shadows against the low
grey sky the still lake refuses
to mirror. Late storms have swept
the gravel from the beach, leaving
powder sand. Derelict beach chairs
tilt against the skeletons of barbecues.
Later, the tattered hammock whips
in a cold north wind. Tiny crystals
chatter against the window like the dry
whisper of rats' feet on a granary floor.
I split birch, imagining the smell
my tobacco obliterates. Inside, your fire
drives the cold into the corners
of the room. A few dull flies
roused from their winter sleep
drift like bombers towards the fireplace.
You are tentative, measuring an area
you can trust, avoiding corners
where the ghost hands of my wife
still hover like silent gulls drifting
across the window. I want to tell you
that the lift of your breasts
as you draw in breath can stun me
like the sudden rise of mallards
in the marsh, that the curve of your body
as you bend over the sink is a landscape
I rooted in my mind before I ever saw you.
When I draw the swede saw across white
logs, I think of the small swell

of your belly, and I forget my soft hands
scraped by the handle. It is not only
fire that makes this room warm.
This is a love song: humming-birds
fireweed, warblers in the willows,
sun on the hot sand, raspberries
in the undergrowth, marsh marigolds,
black currants. All the greens of summer.
You. The lake is choked by ice crystals.
The waves are sluggish, slow. You
are inside, standing by the fire.
Outside, I split birch.

Waking Dreaming

The birdsong that awakens me each morning
fills the air with hostile threats, though
I'd like to think of it as music. Birds
aren't the kind of things you want to fear.
Still, these are cries of warning or of lust
whatever the melody. The politics of nature
you might say, and the shadow of the hawk
gliding over meadow and marsh would prove
you right. Night's not much better. Then
bird cries speak of certain death. The nest
discovered, the silent pounce of this
or that predator: skunk, weasel, fox,
it doesn't matter, one death is equal
to another. But I wanted to say that
I awoke for whatever reason to the song
of birds and the sound of waves pounding
on the shore out of a dream I can't remember
but there was something of you in it,
and something of death, and something of the taste
of ashes. An omen I suppose. Still,
the lessons of nature are much too harsh
to mean anything at all. So when you get here
tonight, if the traffic hasn't been too bad
and you're not too tired, I'll tell you another
dream of women with baskets on their heads
and a snake between them and the well.

Let Me Tell You

When the drapes were drawn
light flooded from the east:
another dawn. The red sun
humped out of the lake
like any whale. Seagulls
proved their industry
clearing the beach
of the night's harvest of insects.

The accident of the red sun
sitting on the lake's horizon
was a textbook illustration:
circles have tangents. The gulls
wheeling and screaming
in the sky didn't matter.

It could have been a grey dawn.
Rain might have splattered on the window.
The gulls might have gone south
or north for that matter.
The point is they were there.

That's for you. A circle
may be touched at any of its points
by a straight line, a horizon.

When I walked to the water's edge
naked (there was no one there)
the breeze was cold on my skin.
The gulls were still there
but the sun had freed itself
from the lake and gone looking
for other horizons. Lost.

It will be back. The sun
always returns. But I may not
be there to see it. The gulls
may be circling some field
or other gulls may be. That's all.
I was there, the sun and the gulls
were there. I thought you should know.

Knowing Is Never Enough

Even after walking three miles
under a light rain from the stone grey sky
finding you here, your hair stringy from the rain
is almost more than I can bear. Already it has been
a morning full of miracles. Four kildeer's eggs
nestled in the gravel of the beach, a nest of tent
caterpillars in a world of foamy gauze, beaded
with rain, a nuthatch clowning on a dead tree stump.
And there were more, more miracles than I can number,
the pale green of early leaves, the screaming chorus
of gulls, orange ladybugs clinging to the rocks
and now you. That you should be sitting in a lawnchair,
your green robe soaked by rain is a gift.
And of course there is the mystery of why you should
have done it at all, I mean, sit there in the rain
waiting for miracles to come to you, while I
was out hunting. Still, I'm not going to ask,
just in case there might be an answer
when I'd rather think you merely needed rain.

Imaginary Love Poem

I imagine myself at the window, watching
the slow looping flight of the imagined bird

pelican perhaps, or gull. In the distance
cormorants hunched on the rocks near the point.

Nearer, the grey lake blends with the grey sky
brown sand, black twig. I wait for the other

(lover, no doubt), a focus for yearning
a point of desire, the absent *you* on the page.

Nothing can happen. Only the buzz of a fly
the scratch of a pencil, things which define

the silence. A distant rumble of thunder
the intimations of loss. Nothing can happen.

My imagined self might move from the window,
the birds gone now, the lake out of sight.

I might read the ashtray for signs, open
a bottle of beer, reach for a glass,

listen for the crush of gravel, the whine
of a motor, hoping it might be you.

Song

Listen carefully.
This welter of words
will not say what I mean.
A green dream
remembered for its green
is as elusive
as what I have to say.
So this:
Your crystal voice
inhabits my head
the way it hovers
in the high
corners of the chapel
above the altar.
You breathe in
and breathe out:

> a flight of birds
> a swell of waves
> a' dream of order
> like a glass globe
> so thin you see it only
> where it scatters light.

Here in this breaking world
where everything is bruised
you draw into yourself
the wounded air
and make it whole.

Freefall

It always begins this way
the wet body slipping   freefall
the first touch of cold wind
the coming of night
strong coffee in the morning
after nights you don't want to remember
tension lurks in the corners
of every room   wind gets into the house
through the cracks around the door
something gets into the house
something wraps itself around the raw
edge of feeling   there are stains on the silver
teaspoons no rubbing will remove
the picture on the television is beginning
to blur   it is spring   the sun is here
longer but the days are getting shorter
the oranges are without taste   the enemy
has pulled his troops back and we don't know
whether to advance or retreat   our arms
hang by our sides   our hands turn
in gestures of dismay   our skin sticks
to the frozen door handle of the car
there are too many sundogs   too many
ice crystals to count   something is
in the air   the animals smell it
and are gone

Berry Picking

And so I went berry picking
though it wasn't allowed
and it looked like rain.
A storm, in fact,
it looked like a storm
and, yes, maybe I was a little drunk
or it only felt like that
but I've picked berries before
and I know that the bush is thick
and there's cobwebs and thorns
and branches that swing
back across your face.
But I know too that berries are sweet
though the juice gets on your hands
and on your lips and you can't get it off.
But it was the season, the right time
when they're ripe and full of juice
so it's this and it's that
if you fear rain, you can't pick berries.

And so I went berry picking
and, yes, the bush was thicker
than I remembered, and I kept thinking
there was something else I had to do
and, yes, there were cobwebs and thorns
and though it didn't rain, it might rain yet
it can always rain.

So
Just where the berries begin
I picked one tree and took the berries home
rattling in the bottom of my pail
and left the rest hanging
on the sweet red trees.

Now I'm out here in the field
where you can see for miles
if there's anything to see.
It's getting late and there's a chill
in the wind coming from the north
but I might make it home, wondering
who will pick my berries now.

Roses

I could, of course, tell you about the roses,
pale pink along the sides of country roads.
Choosing a single petal, I might plaster it
on the windshield, an index to the self
I'd have you know. It's not that easy. I am not
the kind of man you might associate with roses.
Hulking my hung-over rumpled body out into the glare
of Winnipeg winter, the first raw cigarette raking
my throat, I might be Ulysses, back from too many wars
or Byron, alive after all and growing old in Greece.
I make too many people think of bears. I am always
unprepared, always surprised, taken unawares
by what's already common knowledge. You want to snap
your fingers at me. All this is prelude so you'll know
when I begin to talk of roses, they will be roses
long ago dead, withered by the sides of roads
I haven't walked in years. But there were roses once.
They bloomed in nineteen fifty-six and may
have gone on blooming since. I wouldn't know.
But since it's winter now, and time for promises
after the snow, I'll take you to Thermopylae and Troy,
and later to a place where roses grow.

In the Marshes

1.

I have been
all day in the marshes
watching

bitterns stiff
as the reeds
they hide in

redwings at the edges
leaning
into the wind

cormorants
in their comic
flight

you only see
those things
you can name

2.

the sun this morning
rose blood red
out of the lake

cattails marigolds
pinecone
willow gall

I am assigning
names
to the things I know

looking for a sign
looking in the marshes
for a trace of you

these marshes
rich with life
speak your absence

3.

my searching eyes
violate
small private lives

the muskrat swimming
near the creek's shore
on the far side

a raft of white pelicans
fishing in the lagoon
in shallow water

you smiled at me
this morning
then you were gone

I took heart at that smile
listened
for my name

4.

iris and fringed gentian
purple
in the heart of this marsh

a hawk swoops
his wings
a perfect vee

the morning was blue and green
the afternoon was orange
now it is dusk

from the high dike road
I can see
a light in the window

if I call your name
perhaps
you will be there

The Wrong Season

The light October haze
across the bay blurs
the outline of the town.
Franklin gulls
drift on the surface
of the lake or lift
and are carried
to the fishing boats
ghosts against
the absent horizon.

The hollow bump of oars
the squeal of oarlocks
a distant outboard's roar
reverberate in the flannel
of this haze which ought
to muffle but does not.
You on this log are looking
outwards, your binoculars
fixed on the fishermen's
nets dragged across the prow.

You are a study yourself
blue runners, T-shirt,
faded jeans, your hair
loose to the wind
the log you have chosen
to sit on. Once
this might have been
a love poem. I could have
found a reason in the Franklin
gulls, the oar's pull
the white October haze.

It must be the wrong season.
Here with my awkward coffee cup
the cat beside me on the beach
I am blinded by your far-seeing
binocular eyes, the fat red sun
climbing the southern sky.
I could try it. I could
say that I love you, but I know
words spoken over water must be clear
and in this muffled haze you might not hear.

Lightning

lightning has split the ash
that slants between our window
and the lake   the leaves survive
proof that the lean tree lives
when you didn't expect it   loss
is never a certain thing   waxwings
dive from its branches into our glass
window drawn by the false lake
false sky   blur of reflected green
they cannot know, reading
the world they have always thought
was there   but the lightning was real
the tree is riven   split   knowing
it was an accident doesn't help
it isn't a moral question   and so
I've torn a bedsheet twisted tight
and tied the halves together
neat and clean   hoping they will
not hemorrhage bright and green

Stormcloud

the black clouds massed in the north-west
are this evening's text   a storm with
all its portents: ruptures in the fabric
of our tight stretched lives   another
name for pain   something as simple as that

when the boat sinks you cling to what you can
a mast   an oar   whatever's near to you
it doesn't matter who's at fault or why
it's far too late for that   you sink or else

you surface   amazed that the world remains
black clouds   grey sky   the wind that seems
to have been blowing far too long

you look for mushrooms   learn the names of trees
you count the cattails in the scum-filled ditch
and you are happy   the dogwood blossoms
drip onto the grass just where the pathway ends

the massed black clouds are nothing more than clouds
they may not mean a storm   or if they do
it might slip over somewhere to the west
but once you know what drowning might be like
you cling to something and you don't let go

A Violation: The Heart's Reply

What the green world
blade and leaf
disguises

under a black sky
lightning
over the lake

the green and silver
flash of fish

the coyote's moonsong
demi-quaver

green willow
red willow

the water's lyric
the heart's reply

bats in the early dusk
lake and river
night

sun's reflection
camera's lie

the tree's rot
the flicker's entry
a violation

green willow
red willow
green

leafcurl
the bee's insistence

green willow
red willow
green

the bee's insistence
the heart's reply

blade and leaf
lake and river
the heart's reply

under a black sky
the coyote's moonsong
lightning

in the early dusk
bats
in the green world

sun's reflection
demi-quaver

a violation
the heart's reply

green willow
the tree's rot
red willow

over the lake
the black sky

sun's reflection
a violation

the heart's reply

the heart's reply

green willow

a violation

in the early dusk

the bee's insistence

demi-quaver

red willow

flash of fish

the heart's reply

a violation

the green world

leafcurl

red willow

the flicker's entry

the heart's reply

a violation

lake and river

the heart's reply

a violation

SELECTED LYRICS

Intensive Care

wired to the soft emphatic pump
in the soft-lit always early
morning room you breathe pure pain

your bruised and damaged body
answers the electric insistence
with its own erratic pump

you are my mother   they have
torn out your heart   damaged
your lungs   sewn you together again

there are pipes in your throat
liquids drip through clear plastic
numbered and counted in red

you cannot whisper   your mouth
shapes round words that are lost
in the mask's gauzy hiss

I ought to be angry   now
is the time I should weep
for your flesh and my own

I wish I could speak   I wish
you could answer   I need to hear
words in my mother's tongue

in this green room the pulse
of my loving is lost in the music
of metal and plastic and flesh

I am yearning for magic to draw
you toward me   to bind us together
to fasten us heart to heart

In December

Rabbits   in December snow
crouch silent under pines
frightened by the creak of frost
cracked branches, the soft plop
of snow falling from needles
nudged by the wind.

They are as still as china rabbits
on a lawn. As invisible
as they would want to be.
They do not fear hawks
owls or foxes or even
the soft lead of .22 shells
flowering in their palpitating hearts.

Or not the way you'd think, anyway.
Theirs is no focussed fear
no sense that this or that
is dangerous. Fear is what they live
like air, say, that surrounds them.

They cry like babies when you kill them
or when a hawk does. They huddle
in the corner of a cardboard box
when you catch them and bring them
home to eat lettuce and carrots
and they die when you hold them.

But just now they are dancing
in the December snow. Playing
you might think, but their
little hearts are pounding
blood in their ears
and behind their eyes
and later, when a hawk
or a hunter has been by
blood on the white December snow.

The Brother

Me and my brother went into the forest
under the arching spruces where it was dark
with shavings of sunlight on the needle's bed
and there was a cow's skull, I remember,
under the dank willows. Cow's skull,
squirrel's bones, the feathers of birds.
He went home early, my brother I mean
because there was something he had to do,
but I never came out of that forest,
and though I have travelled, I am there still.
Now it is time to go back, time to discover
that brother who suffers from too much sunshine
and who will be searching, I know, under
the arching spruces, under the cow's skull,
under the squirrel's bones, the feathers of birds.

The Joggers

Legs pumping, the heart
ridiculous in its exertions
we circle the concrete track.
Outside, the arterial clog
of traffic wafts white plumes
of exhaust in still winter air.
We yearn backward in time
forward to a finish line
of our own making. Intense,
we count and forget our laps,
listen to the coursing of blood
in veins we are not usually
aware of, discover the ticking
of organs whose names we know
but not their places. Backwards
we run toward some vanished
vision of perfectibility
to some lost innocence.
Alone on the crowded track
we jostle and grunt, finding
a pain that is sweeter than sackcloth
or ashes. The sweet messy
clockwork of our bodies
counting out rhymes that become
more meaningless with every shapely round.
Until, and when it's over
it is always less than we expected,
we round that final curve
to our lonesome victories
our garland of sweaty laurels
and purification by water.
Then with virtuous limps
and muscles stretched by holy
yearning we put on our other

lesser selves with our parkas
and overshoes, and enter,
a little taller, that other
amorphous world where we are not
separate from things.

Harve

Out of this blur of pain, Harve,
the train carries me to Toronto,
your yearning search for guilt
a resonating voice in rooms
already half empty. Children's toys
litter the cold rooms. Your wife's
absent hand waves a cold blessing
over the empty spice rack, the naked
squares on walls where pictures hung.
And you go on talking, telling me
where you might have predicted lightning,
wanting to have failed where there was no failure.
There is nothing you could have done.
So I conjure the future:
sea nymphs, wood nymphs, women
with white bodies, obedient and healthy,
loving you in ways you have always suspected
you should have been loved. Your wound
is raw in the scotch filled room.
You are going to be generous. Your love
is going to survive deep treachery. You
are going to be a model for abandoned husbands.
Your children are beautiful, and you are giving
them as a gift, a net, a hoop. Whatever.
And I want to tell you to rage, to bay
at the moon, to confess endlessly to your
married friends (smug in their loveless unions.
The men will be self-satisfied and afraid.
The women will stroke your head during
Masterpiece Theatre. Later, they will make love
lovelessly. That's some revenge.)
And I am on the train to Toronto
giving advice I have no right to give.
My wife is in some bar, somewhere, with some
(no doubt) contemptible lover. My lover

is telling her suspicious father of my virtue.
My bewildered children loving where they can.
But I've been a priest before, and a good one too
as priests go. A superficial sureness
is my strength. Wood nymph, sea nymph, girls
with high firm breasts, women who can
make you mad, these I can conjure, and that's
something, that's not a lie, they're there.
But a child's cry, a head heavy on the pillow
beside you is something else. Some ways
the greasy peas, the slip on the shower rod
are worth it, though they can't last.
If she hadn't left you Harve, time would have
taken her. Ripeness is your disaster. Loss
at the moment when you had what you wanted.
It's harder when you're blameless, Harve,
when all the women you know would have you,
when your rival is unworthy, and you are
innocent and white as the knights in the stories
your wife loves and you hate. And so,
I counsel vice, Harve, blows at the kingdom
of ideals, lost mornings vomiting over the porch,
exotic diseases, fists through the walls,
injured animals. Variations on the theme
of death. It's not much, but it's all
I have to offer.

On the Dock at Gimli

Begin:
>   Against a wet and hollow sky
>   grey water
>   high pillars of the pier
>   an easy heave of waves

Begin again:
>   Where the curve of the breakwater
>   thrusts against the pier
>   old fishing sheds   the scattered skiffs
>   grey too   or barn red/pocked
>   with flakes and curls of paint

Moving closer now:
>   The pier itself
>   its heavy planks
>   the bump and heave of boats   rain
>   and small pools of water

A figure in the landscape:
>   An Indian girl   her long black hair
>   and heavy swollen belly
>   let her stand shivering on the pier
>   on the boat beside her a fisherman
>   older and with four days' growth of beard
>   let him be drunk
>   as in fact he was

The action (take one):
>   The man   grey bearded   shouts
>   what might have been a curse (he stumbles)
>   the girl tilts forward hands on hips
>   something/despite the swollen belly/draws
>   the grey man moves
>   his gnarled his bitter face his grey hand
>   fills the screen

Interlude:
    The girl lies crumpled
    wet   in the water on the pier
    the sound of weeping
    grey pier   grey water
    and the grey and empty sky

And now again begin:

The Equestrienne

in her cool costume
black jacket   black pants   tight boots
the equestrienne rides
her docile
mount

her neatness denies
his wild mane:
the disorder
his gallop might take

around she goes
orderly
taking the jumps:
her sharp sense of pattern
is tight in the reins

and yet there is passion
in all of this shaping:
she takes
what she needs

and when it's all over
and time for the judges
her costume is rumpled
there is sweat on her eyelids:
wind ruffles her hair

How My Crippled Uncle Could Run

How my crippled uncle could run
dance hobbledehoy over fences
caper   his shrivelled leg aloft
his clutching claw hand grasping at the air
he held armloads of air
caught invisible supports
and bobbed ducked danced
oh but he could run

And he could pick berries
chokecherries high on the bushes he dragged to earth
puckering his mouth
spitting the hard big stones.
Saskatoons purpled his mouth
and he knew where the big sweet gooseberries were
raspberries and black currants
and in the fall   cranberries crabbed
like the hand that picked them
and carried them home in hundred pound short sacks
bucking and weaving and dodging.

He wheezed and he panted
but always he ran.
Cursing and crying   he whirled through my youth.
I followed on sure feet
lost in the willows that whipped closed behind him
mired in swamps he refused to go round.
I tried to keep up with the whirl of his cursing but couldn't.
He sucked from the teats of the cows he was milking
then chased them to pasture
· hopping and shouting   he sang and he cursed
how he danced

Duck Hunting

Once,
I remember,
out in a duck blind
where the marshes meet the lake
near the old dike:
it was early,
and you leaned to the north, my brother
searching for movement in the slow unfolding sky.
I sat behind you with my gun
drawn by the broad innocence of your back
to say:
I will go over and hunt from the reeds
by the edge of the dike.
And I went.

Let me explain.
I know why Cain murdered his brother
and carried his curse.
He could not bear that Abel, whom he loved,
should be so innocent,
and so very vulnerable that anything that passed
could strike him down,
and so he killed him,
saving him with love.

And so I stood in the reeds by the old dike
thigh deep in the cold water
shooting the small, quick, blue-winged teals,
and endlessly killing my brother.

Dreaming of a Father   Lahr Germany   February 14 1978

My father tells me
                    this house will not stand
His carpenter's hands
are knotted   veined
he has always loved too hard
holding and handling
he would never abandon
his building   never say
                    this is done

Now here in my half-built
house he is standing   touching
the joists and the rafters
testing the floor and the stringers   checking
the cracks in the concrete
he says   *this house will not stand*
                     none of your houses will stand

English Department

And you want to say
what do I care about all
the lily white girls
seduced in the back seats of cars
by drunken louts
who can hardly wait for it
to be over so that they
can brag to their buddies
all those fathers' daughters
or else
what do I care about
all those kittens drowned
in sacks   floating
in polluted rivers
by all those daughters' fathers
what do I care about
burned bodies in some desert
hijacked airplanes
going places I would never go
the fractured sanctuary
of embassies   children
exploding in a bus
troops and tanks in Afghanistan
murdered priests
raped nuns   black men
crawling deep under ground
in South African mines
the world's harvest of vomit
in torture camps in Chile
or Chad   bruised genitals
missing fingers   all
the jarring meetings
of metal and flesh
what do I care
about violence and sudden disaster

here where envy and petty malice
drift down grey corridors
betrayal happens behind closed doors
and you never know   snide whispers
and soft lust waft like
the odour of chrysanthemums
across a field of decaying hope
what do I care   here
where only acid rain
slow cancer and the heart's
declining pump threaten
what do I care is
what you want to say.

Green Girl

a girl in green
twirls to the heavy beat
of the battering drum
the plucked guitar

she is empty dancing
the thing that was in her
drawn through the plastic tubes
that drained to a porcelain sink

and now she is dancing
her dark hair whirls
red/green in the flashing lights
her green dress twists
her body strains
her stomach tight and shrunk
last night she wept
for the thing that was in her
that will never dance
but the guitars snap
and the big drum pounds
and tonight she is dancing
drunk

That Girl

That girl with her body stretching
draws her boyfriend near. She
wants to go. He has been drinking
beer. He wants the fuzzed soft lights
the deep male drone of talk. She
presses her breast against his shoulder.
Something stirs but to leave
would be loss. He whispers just
one more. She arches her back
ruffles her hair with long fingers
stares at the boy at the next table.
He crosses his legs, turns back
to male chatter. Her head leans back.
She looks at the lights in the ceiling
as if they were stars.

DESCARTES & DICK

RENE DESCARTES AND DEADWOOD DICK: A SENTIMENTAL POEM IN SEVERAL CANTOS CONTAINING A THRILLING LOVE STORY, A NARROW ESCAPE FROM HOSTILE INDIANS AND A NUMBER OF PERTINENT PHILOSOPHICAL OBSERVATIONS ALL TOGETHER WITH A GUEST APPEARANCE BY THE AUTHOR HIMSELF.

The river is dry:

>   a school of words
>   swimming between
>   the empty banks

I went to talk to a poet
There was no one home

>   I put the question to Descartes:
>   Rene, I said, I think...
>   He took away my ballpoint pen.
>   Avoid iambics, he said

In the trees along the river
the birds were singing in Latin
I picked out a *Colaptes Auratus*
a *Dendroica Magnolia* and a couple of *Paradidae.*
There may even have been an *Arenaria Interpres,*
I can't remember

I looked for a sign
I couldn't find one anywhere

>   Let me put it to you this way, I told her
>   No   Not that way, she said, not yet

She was waiting for a sign

The bottom of the river was covered with fossils
                                (actually, they weren't fossils yet
                                they were only rotting fish
                                waiting to harden)

Rene, I said
I think you're being
awfully selfish

                Rene said I know that
                but it's been a hard winter

                                Let me take you away from all this
                                I told her

                                Later
                                she said

The river was dry

*He was of about medium stature, and as straight and square
shouldered as an athlete. His complexion was nut-brown, from
long exposure to the sun; hair of the hue of a raven's wing, and
hanging in long straight strands down his back; eyes black and
piercing as an eagle's; features well molded, with a firm resolute
mouth and prominent chin.*

Where is the girl, I asked them
I heard her calling

                Haven't seen a sign of her
                Haven't seen hide nor hair of her
                Sorry, there's nobody home

On the edge of the horizon
I can see a thin line of smoke
Somebody else's signal

> Rene, I said
> you're putting the cart before the horse
> go on out and get laid

> Rene told me
> I think
> I will

Harder Rene, she said
I am, he answered
Ardour
I am, I think

> *I calkytlate 'twern't no* he *as made them*
> *squawks. Sing out like a bellerin' bull, now, and*
> *et are more of less likely—consider'bly more of*
> *less 'n less of more—that she will respond.*

A poet sent me a sonnet
I gave it to the museum
for their collection

> Have you ever written a sonnet Rene, I asked
> Not me   I'm too full of self-doubt, he answered

Well, let me put it to you this way
No, not that way   It hurts

He put the spurs to his spirited animal and the next instant was dashing wildly over the sunlit plain. On—on dashed the fearless youth, mounted on his noble steed, his eyes bent forward, in a sharp scrutiny of the plain ahead, his mind filled with wonder that the cries were now growing more distinct, and yet not a first glimpse could he obtain of the source whence they emanated.

Q. Could I please speak with Mr. Descartes?
A. Sorry, he's gone west. Poor Rene.

Grove: To the left I found the first untilled land. It stretched
         far away to the west, overgrown with scrub-willow,
         wolf-willow and symphoricarpus. (*Over Prairie Trails*)

Arnason: Symphoricarpus?

(The birds were singing in Latin. Jug Jug, they sang. Cocoricoco.)

Well let me put it to you this way
Sorry, I have a headache

> *Stood there, to behold a sight that made the blood boil in his veins. Securely bound with her face toward a stake, was a young girl, of perhaps seventeen summers, whom, at a glance, one might surmise was remarkable pretty.*
> *She was stripped to the waist, and upon her snow white back were numerous welts from which trickled diminutive rivulets of crimson. Her head was drooped against the stake to which she was bound, and she was evidently insensible.*

I've got something in my eye.
Here, I'll get it out with the corner of my handkerchief.
Good, it's gone. What was it?
A mote, I think, though it may have been a beam.
I couldn't tell.

Blood on the saddle
Blood on the ground
Great big globs
Of blood all around

> The river is dry, Rene,
> it's out of water
> only the banks to show us
> where the river once ran

Sign here on the dotted line ....
> (At last, a sign)

I found a lot of things on the riverbed:
> An arrowhead
> A copper kettle
> A sonnet (in almost perfect working order
> needing only a new couplet and
> a couple of iambs   you can
> get those anywhere)

Jug Jug Jug

Deadwood Dick then hastened to approach the insensible captive,
and, with a couple sweeps of his knife, cut the bonds that held
her to the torture stake. Gently he laid her on the grass and
arranged about her half nude form...
> Jug Jug Jug
> Cocoricoco

(a shy little prairie maid)

        ...*the garments Sitting Bull's*
warriors had torn off, and soon he had the satisfaction of seeing
her once more properly clothed.

"Fear not, miss:" and the youth
gently supported her to a sitting
posture. "I am a friend, and your
cruel captors have vamosed. Lucky
I came along just as I did, or it's
likely they'd have killed you."

"Oh. Sir, how can I ever thank
you for rescuing me from those
merciless fiends!" and the maiden
gave him a grateful glance. "They
whipped me terribly!"

The ring rang doo
Oh what is that
All round and firm
Like a pussycat

Rene, I shouted, help me:

> I am
> lost
> I am
> bewildered
> I am
> be
> wild
> ered

      Bugger off, Rene replied. We don't need no sissy
poets in this man's land.
          (Oh the sun shines bright on pretty...)
          Jug Jug Jug
               Cocoricoco

My aunt said, David, our car is in the garage. I wonder if
you could whip me home? I went to get my whip, but by
the time I got back she was gone.

> **$500. Reward: For the apprehension
> and arrest of a notorious young
> desperado who hails to the name of
> Deadwood Dick. His present
> whereabouts are somewhat contiguous
> to the Black Hills. For further
> information and so forth, apply
> immediately to Hugh Vansere "At
> Metropolitan Saloon"**

*Slowly, over and over, Deadwood
Dick, outlaw, road agent and
outcast, read the notice and then
a wild sardonic laugh burst from
behind his mask—a terrible,
blood-curdling laugh that made
even the powerful animal he
bestrode start and prick up its
ears.*

(all covered with hair)

prick
up its
ears?

Jug Jug Jug Jug Jug Jug Jug Jug Jug Jug Jug Jug Jug Jug Jug
Cocoricocococoricocococoricocococoricocococoricocococoricococorico

Rene, I said, give me a sign.
Give up poetry, he said. It's a mug's game.

70

"Had it not been for you, sir no
one but our god knows what
would have been my fate. Oh! sir,
what can I do, more than to
thank you a thousand times to
repay you for the great service you
have rendered me?"

(and split in two)

Let me put it to you
this way?

JugJugJugJugJugJugJugJugJugJugJugJugJugJugJugJugJugCocoricoco

(the breezes sighing)

And then in the summer of seventy-four
It rained and it rained till it flooded our door
And the river was rising, it flooded the bed
Where young Deadwood Dick and the maiden he'd wed
Were lying together in heavenly bliss
And that's all the story, except just for this:

(The horse was drowned, the house was swept away
the birds gave up Latin, Descartes was drowned
there wasn't a sign left. It was a hell of a flood.)